Finding Joy in Transitions

Blooming in the
Seasons of Change

PRAISE FOR *FINDING JOY IN TRANSITIONS*

"There is nothing like having a pillar of strength and a personal champion when we are going through a life transition. That is exactly who Sam is for so many people. This book captures Sam's deep understanding of what it takes to thrive in our personal challenges. Her immense experience as a women's life coach shines through. Readers will enjoy how intelligently practical yet empathic it is. This is where the value of the book truly lies: It delivers the essence of Sam and that transformational magic she brings into her work with her clients and teams."

— **Lin Tan**
Master Certified Coach, International Coach Federation
Director of Training, Collective Change Institute
President (2020), ICF Singapore Chapter

"What makes this volume carry weight are the real stories that inspired each chapter. I especially enjoy the questions which Sam has thoughtfully curated at the end of each chapter. They may look simple, but they could be just what is needed to give us that much needed reflective pause. *Finding Joy in Transitions* is definitely not a book to be finished in one reading."

— **Gloria Arlini**
Deputy Director (Strategy & Policy), National Volunteer & Philanthropy Centre

"As a coach, Sam has helped me work through sticky decision points in my entrepreneurial journey so I could view them through a new lens. I am so glad that she has written this book which will help us reframe transitions from difficult challenges to joyful opportunities in a thoughtful, accessible and practical manner. I can definitely see myself pulling this book out over the years when changes happen and I need to look for a new perspective!"

— **Toni Chan**
Founder and Creative Director, August Society

"I have known Sam for several years professionally. She is a deeply empathetic and highly skilled coach, and someone who holds herself and others to the highest degree of integrity. As the managing director of a global coaching firm, Sam is always my go-to coach in helping organisations and leaders manage transitions. Her feedback from clients is always positive. Sam has the unique ability to be caring while holding the complexity of transitions from both a psychological and practical perspective in order to offer pragmatic, solutions-oriented support. This book is an extension of her knowledge, experience and words of wisdom—a must-read for anyone going through their own transition."

— **Saba Hasanie**
Managing Director, OSC Leadership Performance

"Sam has helped me navigate difficult decisions in my professional and personal life. I have benefited from her deep empathy and she has helped me find the courage to handle tough conversations and have the clarity to move forward. As a reader, this book does exactly that: It feels as close as it can be to having conversations with Sam on important life decisions. May you also find calmness in approaching transitions as you build the confidence in embracing change."

— **Yi Ning Lim**
Marketing professional

"I thoroughly enjoyed reading *Finding Joy in Transitions*. What struck me most was the way Sam was able to capture so much experiential wisdom on the different transition scenarios and put them together in such a delightful and effortless read. Anyone could benefit from this book as we all go through transitions in some stages of life and having this book will allow us to make sense of the anxieties associated with the changes and take inspired action to move forward with ease."

— **Suman Balani, PCC**
Managing Director, Flourish Consulting Pte Ltd

"*Finding Joy in Transitions* is a wonderful resource for the many stages of transition and change that we find ourselves experiencing in life. I love that the chapters can easily be read in any order. The Reflection for Clarity questions at the end of each chapter make it especially practical and useful. If you find yourself stuck on how to move through a change in your life, I highly recommend this book."

— **Susan Sadler, PCC**
Founder, Sadler Communications LLC

Finding Joy in Transitions

Blooming in the Seasons of Change

LAI HAN SAM

Candid Creation Publishing

First published 2021

Candid Creation Publishing books are available through most major bookstores in Singapore. For bulk order of our books at special quantity discounts, please email us at enquiry@candidcreation.com.

FINDING JOY IN TRANSITIONS

Blooming in the Seasons of Change

Author:	Lai Han Sam
Publisher:	Phoon Kok Hwa
Editor:	Zoe Toh
Layout:	Geelyn Lim
Cover design:	Patricia Alix
Published by:	Candid Creation Publishing LLP 167 Jalan Bukit Merah #05-12 Connection One Tower 4 Singapore 150167
Website:	www.candidcreation.com
Email:	enquiry@candidcreation.com
Facebook:	www.facebook.com/CandidCreationPublishing
ISBN:	978-981-14-9679-0

Names: Lai, Han Sam.
Title: Finding joy in transitions : blooming in the seasons of change / Lai Han Sam.
Description: Singapore : Candid Creation Publishing, 2021.
Identifiers: OCN 1249621320 | ISBN 978-981-14-9679-0 (paperback)
Subjects: LCSH: Self-help techniques. | Life change events. | Adjustment (Psychology).
Classification: DDC 158.1--dc23

To God, Jesus and Mother Mary, without whom I would not have survived and thrived.

To the love of my life:
强, for your unwavering love, support and belief in me.

To my children:
宇, who birthed a mother in me as I birthed him and inspired me stay true to myself;

宙, who gifted me her love and her tenacity in making all things possible;

心, whose love for animals, humour and curiosity made me laugh; and

思, whose questions opened my heart and mind to endless possibilities.

To all those in transition, you are not alone.

Contents

Foreword

"Who am I? Because the answer, like the seasons, constantly, subtly, inevitably changes. And who it is you are today, is not the same person you will be tomorrow."
– Richelle E. Goodrich

Having known Sam for a long time, I am well-acquainted with her work as a coach and advisor. Over the years, I have watched her professional journey go through transition after transition. Each new role brought out a fresh level of strength in her as she navigated through the external changes required to adapt to the new norms. Over time, I also got to know Sam better on a personal basis and was introduced to her journey as a mother, wife and daughter. Again, she impressed me with her realistic positivity. She always faced adversity with a positive enthusiasm and a desire to make every challenge a learning opportunity.

Slowly, I started to understand Sam's calming presence as she reflected a structured and organised method of breaking down problems for herself and for others. It was her ability to coach effectively that made her one of the best programme managers, supporting the reintegration of back-to-work female talents hired through the various Mums@Work projects. Many of the ladies who benefitted from Sam's guidance gave positive feedback on her work and praised her for being their pillar of support during challenging times.

Knowing that Sam has put her lifetime of experiences and work into a book truly excites me.

As we go through the journey of life, nothing brings greater comfort than having someone guide us to make better decisions by asking pertinent questions and sharing stories of encouragement. This book feels like an extension of Sam's warmth and support as a coach. As you flip through the pages of this book, you can almost imagine Sam sitting next to you in an armchair, wearing a big friendly smile, asking you the questions set out in each Reflection for Clarity section. These questions will help you dig deep. These questions will support the way you frame your life challenges. These questions will also partner you to make decisions that will help your growth.

Begin your journey of self-discovery with *Joy in Transitions* as your companion navigator through life.

Sher-li Torrey
Founder, Mums@Work Singapore
Founder, Career Navigators Singapore

Preface

"A miracle is a shift in perception from fear to love."
– Marianne Williamson

I always knew there is at least one book in me. The thing that intimidated me the most in writing a book was the fact that I did not think I was worthy enough. I thought that this is my life, my normal, my journey—who would care? Why would anyone need to a book like this? Is this just a self-centred exercise (said my self critic)?

When asked by friends from the Authors' Club, one which we set up to journey, challenge and celebrate our transformation to authors, why I wanted to write this book, I was initially stumped. It was a long-time dream, but I did not have a tangible reason to ground me. It became my first step in discovering my very deep and personal reason for writing this book.

Inspired by a vision creation tool, I modified it to help me get to my "why". What tumbled out of my heart was both surprising and motivating to me.

To become the spark for change, the inspiration to transform, to let my readers know they are not alone and that there is a way.

Reading this again and again moved me enough to write this book. Perhaps my journey can be a beacon of light for others. I do not need to be worthy or perfect. I just needed to share my experience and knowledge with all my imperfections. I can just be me.

This was after a five-year transition journey, followed by another three years of recreating my life and identity from scratch. During this time, I shared my aspirations, my hopes, my dreams, my challenges and my pain to women I met, friends who cared and family who was my rock. I was told that because of what I shared, they dared to dream again and entertain the possibility of change. More importantly, they do not have to stay stuck.

There is a way.

Stuck. It is the most common word my clients say to me. To get out of that stuck-ness was messy and painful for me. It was also a journey of self-discovery and connecting back to my true self and back to God. It was a journey to find the girl who used to sing out loud in public, who lovingly holds space for others to process their pain and who loves ice cream, the girl whom I buried for reason of having to provide for my family. I hid behind that reason for a long time, out of fear. Through this journey, I finally found the courage to choose love despite my fears and create a new beginning.

How to read this book

This is not a typical book. You do not have to read it from cover to cover. This book is also not written to help you learn deeply about transitions.

This book is a lifelong companion. A journey. A dialogue. A conversation.

Finding Joy in Transitions is a partner in the seasons of change you will be experiencing in your life. This pocket guide is created to fit your handbag. It is meant to be whipped out in an instant when you or someone in your life is experiencing a transition. Reading the book will ignite in you strategies to move forward, reflections to deepen your self-awareness and resources to further build your capacity in managing transitions. Each entry takes no more than 5-10 minutes to read.

Even if your personal transition is nothing like the ones depicted in the book, it will still be able to inspire you with ideas, reflections and thoughts to move forward.

It is a book to be shared. It is a book that is meant to be passed around, its pages flipped until they turn yellow, dog-eared and well-used. It is meant to remind you that you are not alone. It gives you a fertile ground to grow on during uncertain times.

There is always a way. Yes.

As you move through the seasons of change and transitions in your life, you know you have something to depend on, to perhaps even thrive in this journey, to know that you can complete transitions with a new beginning, and to have courage, hope and joy.

Disclaimer

This book is not a replacement for mental health support and therapy.

It is a resource to help you think, reflect and find out more about your own personal challenge. It will not solve any of your problems—you have to solve your own problem.

It will not make your transition a breeze. It is a book that will help you reframe and inspire you to get the support you need.

If you experience mental health challenges or if you are unsure if you are experiencing mental health challenges, please reach out to a mental health specialist where you are.

The stories in this book are fictional. Names, characters, businesses, places, events, locales and incidents are either the products of the author's imagination or used in a fictitious manner. Any resemblance to actual persons, living or dead, or actual events is purely coincidental.

May this book be a beacon of light for you. We are in this together.

Change vs Transition

"All changes, even the most longed for, have their melancholy;
for what we leave behind us is a part of ourselves;
we must die to one life before we can enter another."
– **Anatole France**

First things first: Change is not the same as transition.

William Bridges, author of the classic *Transitions: Making Sense of Life's Changes,* wrote: ... changes are driven to reach a goal, but transitions start with letting go of what no longer fits or is adequate to the life stage you are in.[1]

For example, you changed jobs. The change may be quick: You stop going to your old workplace one day and start work at the new workplace the very next day. Your job title changed, you give out new name cards and you simply change your travel route during your morning commute.

However, the onboarding, adjusting, getting to know your new co-workers and new organisational culture, exploring new lunch places... all these take time.

Things are different and things feel different. You will likely experience obstacles, discomfort, and emotional challenges during the adjustment period. After this period, you settle into your new normal comfortably and are more at ease. You know what to expect. You know how to be.

Simply put, change is on the outside while transition is on the inside. They move at different speeds and will not be aligned. Once you have dealt with the change, you have to work on the transition.

What is a transition?

A transition is a multistep and iterative process that supports the re-examination of one's assumptions about identity, capacity and values.[2] It takes time, energy and focus to traverse a transition.

How do transitions happen?

At the pre-transition stage, a trigger happens. A trigger can be anything from losing a job, having a new baby, to moving to another country. A trigger can be perceived to be positive or negative. When that happens, there is a decision to be made to take action to move towards transition.

The decision stage is often the longest, especially if the trigger is negative because you may still be in denial, anger or disappointment. This is the stage most people would be stuck at. It takes time to process the thoughts and feelings that accompany the trigger. Therefore, be gentle with yourself. Ask for help.

However, once the decision is made, you will enter into the transition stage. This begins with accepting that to have new beginnings, you must start with endings. It is about making peace with losing a job, accepting the end of only thinking of yourself or saying goodbye to the country you are leaving.

This is the part of the transition that is most disorienting and frightening for most. It involves leaving what you know and accepting the uncertainty of the future into your life. It is also the most important one. It is only when you let go of the old that you can move towards the neutral zone where the most development work is done.

Pre-transition

Transition

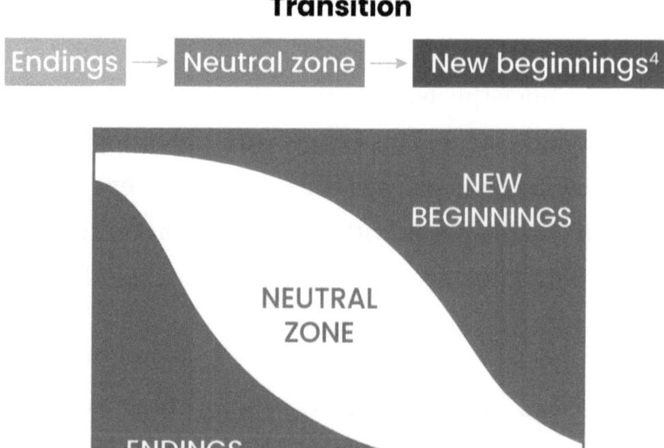

Post-transition

Clarity and development of new identity, capacity and values

What happens in the neutral zone?

The neutral zone is a period of reorganising, resetting and reframing our identity, life and future. It is the time where your thinking changes, your wants and needs transform, and your goals move towards the creation of a new beginning. This stage may be very disorienting and uncomfortable. It is like being thrown into the wilderness with very little semblance of your past life. It can be very painful and stressful.

There is a search for meaning and purpose for the new life. The operating system is still not firm yet and you may feel a bit wobbly, perhaps not dissimilar to visiting a strange country. Yet without moving through this neutral zone, you cannot create your new beginnings.

The neutral zone is hard work.

How can I move through the neutral zone?

There is a lot of inside work when you journey through the neutral zone during a transition. It is extremely helpful to have the ways of being during this process.

By reframing what Linda Rossetti states as the needs

for women in transition in her book *Women and Transition*,[5] they can apply to all transitions for you.

1. Be future focused rather than past focused
The past is part of us and while we cannot change it, we can learn from it and grow from it. However, to be clear, to move through a transition, one cannot stay in the past. You can value the past as part of you, but you must not be limited by it and be focused on discovering the possibilities for the future.

2. Be anchored by a clear view of self-identity
This is the self-awareness and clarity that you have of who you are and what you stand for. During the transition, there will be confusion around your current identity and the identity you are transitioning into, the overlaps and the differences of the two. There is hard work in making sure you have a clear view of your self-identity. Until this is established, you will stay in the neutral zone.

3. Be mindful of your reluctance to go beyond your comfort zone
Do you know what they say about a comfort zone? Nothing grows there. If you want growth and development, you must do something that will challenge you and help you grow bigger and taller. You will feel the force of strong reluctance as you go through the neutral zone, but remember that you are

not alone. Find ways that work for you to get over the inertia of moving towards uncertainty. Overwrite your instinct to move back into your comfort zone.

4. Be respectful of the reality of constraints in your daily life
Remember that life goes on even during a transition. While you are struggling during this period of time, you will still need to put food on the table, complete your work or fulfil your duties as a productive member of society. There will be challenges, no doubt, but this is the reality. The process of transition will not be quick and easy. The ability to understand this and practise self-compassion will go a long way in sustaining the efforts of growth and development. Be patient and kind to yourself.

---

[1] Bridges, William. *Transitions: Making Sense of Life's Transitions.* De Capo Press Lifelong Books, 2004, pp. 128.

[2] Rossetti, Linda. *Women and Transition: Reinventing Work and Life.* Palgrave Macmillan, 2015, pp. 33.

[3] Rossetti, Linda. *Women and Transition: Reinventing Work and Life.* Palgrave Macmillan, 2015, pp. 32.

[4] Bridges, William. *Transitions: Making Sense of Life's Transitions.* De Capo Press Lifelong Books, 2004, pp. 4.

[5] Rossetti, Linda. *Women and Transition: Reinventing Work and Life.* Palgrave Macmillan, 2015, pp. 77.

Life Stage Changes

I Got Married

"There are a hundred paths through the world that are easier than loving. But who wants easier?"
– **Mary Oliver**

Transition Story

I just got married a few months ago and am now living with my husband in our own place. Although all this newness and novelty is exciting and fun, I struggle with adjusting to my new identity, role and routine.

There are so many things I don't know about being a wife and partner. I am not confident about our sexual relationship. I am worried about combining our finances, managing our families (especially our parents) and our different work routines. He wants children, but I am not sure if I am ready. The weight of the new expectations is clouding my judgements daily. I miss my parents and family. I feel so overwhelmed and someone at work says this is normal.

Is it? How can I make this work better for me?

Thinking Differently

While you have embarked on this new adventure, it sounds like you just left your old life and stepped into the stage of merging two lives into one. Since both of you are different individuals, this is going to be a journey rather than a switch turned on after the wedding.

As you and your husband move from one stage of life to another, remember that marriage is always a lifelong work in progress. This is indeed different from what you are familiar with and what is comfortable for you.

While this is a change that was triggered by the both of you, it may still take time and effort to get to the next stage of your lives together. It is important to understand that transitions are different for different people. The main idea is to know and accept that you need to take the time to traverse the wildness of this transition.

Moving Forward

1. Accept that your journey needs to take the time it needs

You will feel uncomfortable for a while, but it does not mean nothing is happening. Everyone experiences marriage differently so do not rush. Allow yourself to take time and make decisions only when you are ready. Take it one step at a time.

2. Share what you need with your loved ones

Since you know that everyone experiences changes differently, help your loved ones understand what you need. Ask for time to adjust and for their help to support and encourage you. This is especially important for your husband as he is also transitioning through married life. You are doing it together, but separately.

3. Implement self-care (extreme even!)

Take care of yourself during this time. It can be routines that would make you happy and contented, like exercising, eating well, meditating, spending time with friends or just having quiet time to yourself. It can also be something simple like watching your favourite television shows or just chilling with a good book.

4. Tackle each challenge one by one

You do not have to handle all the changes and challenges all at once. Prioritise what needs to get done first and then move on to the next item. When there are many things going on at the same time, make sure you ask for help when needed.

5. Keep in contact with friends and family

Even if you cannot physically spend time with your friends and family, a quick phone call or video call can help you feel connected to your support network. Make the effort to visit your parents or go out for a meal with your close relatives. It will help you stay grounded so you can do the inner work of the transition into married life.

6. Talk to someone who is married

Reach out to someone you trust who is married and ahead of you in the marriage journey. Sharing your thoughts, feelings and fears with a mentor can help you alleviate your worries and soothe the rough edges of the transition. If you have friends whose marriage you would like to emulate, arrange for a double date with them and ask them to share their experiences.

Reflection for Clarity

- What are my hopes and dreams for my marriage?

- How can I be a wife to my husband while maintaining my self-identity?

- What can I do to discover new communication skills?

- How can I maintain contact with my family and maintain the sanctity of my marriage?

- Who and what can I depend on to figure this out?

I Just Gave Birth to a Baby

"Birth takes a woman's deepest fears about herself and show her that she is stronger than them."

– **Unknown**

Transition Story

I feel so new to this motherhood gig. My baby is three months old and I still do not feel like a mother. I feel extremely trapped and stifled with the lack of sleep, daily diaper changing and feedings. My husband is very supportive and hands-on, but I am worried about sharing these feelings with him. There is so much guilt and self-loathing, and I feel so inadequate as a mother. Will these feelings ever go away?

I love my baby, but sometimes it is such a burden to me. Even the thought of the baby being a burden is a burden to me! I am always tired and it seems like people around me expect me to know what to do. I don't know and I don't even know what I don't know. I feel so helpless and incompetent so I overcompensate by doing everything myself.

I am worried I may have postnatal blues, but I am ashamed to get it confirmed. I struggle with the thought that there is something wrong with me.

What if people think I am crazy? How can I face my family?

Thinking Differently

Take a breath! You sound like you are totally overwhelmed and burnt out by the new duties, new routines and new expectations of being a mother. You are enough just the way you are.

Like you, many women made the loving decision to bring a precious life to the world. This is one of the most emotional and stressful transitions any woman can make. You are not alone in this journey. While being a parent is one of the most difficult roles you can have, it is also the most rewarding and joyful. We all have different journeys and there is no need to compare.

I know it does not feel like it yet, but that is because you have not processed the ending of your life before you became a mother. There are also the natural hormones that are still cycling through your body. The effects of these hormones vary from woman to woman and can be very powerful. This is biological and thus, we cannot control these natural processes and effects they have on us.

Moving Forward

1. Accept help
You may feel protective and responsible for looking after your baby. If you are overwhelmed, do ask for help. When others offer to help, try to say yes as many times as possible. This will allow you to have the time you need to figure out and accept your role as a mother and your own new identity. Know that around the world, all new mothers need help and support.

2. There are no perfect mothers in the world
They may look perfect, especially on social media, but no one is perfect. Thus, do not compare yourself to other mothers. You are just what your child needs, so relax and do not hold yourself up against impossible standards. It is okay just to be enough. When you relax, your baby will relax too and both of you can enjoy that calming time together. You can then focus on building the new relationship you have.

3. Connect with women you trust

It could be your best friend, your mother or your sister. Spend time with them and confide in them your challenges and feelings. Allow them to support and encourage you in this journey. Those who are mothers may be able to share with you some experiences and what worked or not worked for their own babies. It will also help you feel less alone.

4. Self-care and self-compassion

This is the time to take time to care for yourself, even if it means taking an hour off from baby to be by yourself, doing things you love or just taking a nap. This will refresh you and give you the energy you need to tackle this transition. Be gentle with yourself—there is no need to be perfect. Be mindful of your negative thoughts and counter them when you need to.

5. Seek professional help

If you feel overwhelmed all the time or have feelings that render you paralysed, emotionally or physically, please seek professional help. These people are trained to ask the right questions and are knowledgeable in their field. They will be able to give you the help you need. I know you may be feeling vulnerable and ashamed, but getting help is a form of self-care and self-compassion.

Reflection for Clarity

- What am I grateful for in my life?

- What do I want for my child?

- Who can I be now that I am also a mother?

- What can I do to make my parenting journey a joyful one?

- How can I be a partner with my husband in raising my baby?

All My Kids Left Home

"Your child's life will be filled with fresh experiences.
It's good if yours is as well."
– Dr Margaret Rutherford

Transition Story

I am a mother to three adult children, aged 29 to 34. They have been moving out of our family home one by one over the last few years. This is uncommon in the Asian household as we expect our kids to stay with us until they get married.

While I love seeing their independence and am happy for them to have their own place, I feel lost going from day to day. I still see them weekly, but it is not the same for me. It was still manageable with the first two, but when the last child left home, I felt like I lost my identity as a mother.

I suddenly have so much time on my hands! Even though I work full-time and spend time with my husband, there is an empty spot in my heart. It does not help that my husband does not share my experience as he is more than happy to have them out of the house. He is suggesting all kinds of new activities, but I dread saying yes with this emptiness in my life.

What is happening to me? Is this the empty nest syndrome that people talk about?

Thinking Differently

How wonderful that you have raised three independent and contributing adults! Despite all the hard work, motherhood must have been very meaningful to you. It filled your days and there is always something they need from you.

Now that they have left home, why not start thinking about how you would like to create other types of meaning in your life. There may have been times during their growing up years that you wish you could have some time to pursue your hobbies or passions. Now is the time.

This is a huge milestone and a celebration is due. Taking a moment to recognise this will help you appreciate how far you have come. It is also time to devote more time in yourself and your marriage. Remember, you are still their mother and they will always need you.

Moving Forward

1. Find your purpose
The first half of your life is different from the second half. Most of the first half is about striving and working towards success in work and building finances. In the second half, you would likely want a more meaningful purpose. Reflect and think about what would make you happy during this season of your life.

2. Have new experiences
If you are not sure what you want, try new things. New experiences may spark a light of passion that you were not aware existed. Go for a cooking class, travel to a place you have never been before or attend a charity event. You may meet people or gain experiences that will broaden your thinking and life. The possibilities are endless and life can be really exciting and enriching.

3. Grow yourself
Continue to invest in yourself in terms of knowledge and intellectual progress. Lifelong learning contributes to self-development and self-understanding. You will

find out new things about yourself and others that you did not know before. Perhaps this is the time to pick up a new skill or that certification you have been thinking about.

4. Spend time with other family members and friends
Connecting with your loved ones and spending more time with them is a great way to use the time you have now wisely. It is important to find support and encouragement during this time of transition. Perhaps you will find that sharing of the same experience that your loved ones may have gone through will help you to see things from a different perspective. Start with your husband!

5. Celebrate and enjoy
Accept that this is a changing season in your life. Work on going with the flow and know that this is the purpose of a parent. You want your children to be independent, confident and self-sufficient. This has always been your goal. So, pat yourself on the back for a job well done!

Reflection for Clarity

- How can I fill the second half of my life with meaning?

- What is the state of my relationship with my own parents?

- Who am I really?

- How can I change my perspective of my children to see them as adults?

- What new experiences would I like to have?

I Am Experiencing Menopause

"So many women I've talked to see menopause as an ending. I've discovered that this is your moment to reinvent yourself after years of focusing on the needs of everyone else."

– **Oprah Winfrey**

Transition Story

It started with hot flushes and insomnias. Then, when I could hardly function at work and got really short-tempered, people started to notice the difference in me. Eventually, I had to see my gynaecologist. She did a panel of hormone tests and I was then told I was experiencing menopausal symptoms.

I am only 43 years old so I was shocked. It was too early in my life to have menopause. I hardly heard a word she said about how my bones will get brittle, how my risk of heart disease will increase and whether I wanted hormone replacement therapy. All I felt was the dread and sadness of getting older. Will this affect my relationship with my husband?

I tried to find out more information about menopause from my family and friends. Either they shush me, tell me it is private and told me not to talk about it or they have not experienced it yet. I ended up going on the Internet and scaring myself with the massive amount of information I read.

I know this is an inevitable stage of life, but I am at a loss.

Thinking Differently

Your recognition that this is a transition, an inevitable stage of life, is a good start as you move through it. This is a time to pause, rethink and rediscover how you want your life to look like. Other than handling the physical changes you will experience, do not forget about the emotional and psychological changes you will go through. You can really make this stage the time of your life once you see it differently.

Moving Forward

1. Create a life that will support you physically
Consult with your gynaecologist your options to make your life more comfortable. Whether it is taking up hormone replacement, changing your sleep environment or the supplements you take, you can find a way that will suit you. Remember that you can take charge and be the advocate for yourself and the kind of life you want to live.

2. You are not alone
Unfortunately, menopause is not widely discussed in society and many have very little knowledge about it. If you are unable to find people in your network who can help, online support groups and websites can help you find the support and information you need. Be open and you will find others who are willing to share their journey with you. Do not forget to involve your husband. Help him understand your challenges and what you need so he can also support you.

3. Get psychological support
Just as hormones rage during puberty, so does it happen with menopause. You may struggle to control your emotions and outbursts. It can disrupt your life and relationships if not taken care of. Do not hesitate to search for help and support from a professional counsellor or psychologist. Early intervention can help you to modulate and handle such situations better.

4. This is not your identity

As you journey through menopause, know that it is not you. It is just a stage of life every woman goes through. It does not define who you are and what you stand for. Remember also that this is only temporary and it is definitely not the end!

5. Celebrate and enjoy

Going through menopause can be a new beginning! During this time in your life, you can reinvent yourself and think about what really matters to you. You can take it as a cue from life and pause to find meaning in your journey. Trust the process and go with the flow in creating a new life.

Reflection for Clarity

- How can I reframe this stage of my life positively?

- What quality of life would I want to create for myself?

- How can I support others who are going through the same experience?

- What can I do to set myself up for success?

- How can I embrace this transition?

My Spouse/ Partner is Retiring

"A thriving new beginning can be and should be a time for amazing engagement, growth, connections, contributions and amazing possibilities."
– Lee M. Brower

Transition Story

My husband is going to retire in the next three months. I am so excited for him as I know he has been waiting for this to happen.

While he is looking forward to the nice long break before he decides if he is going to do anything else, I am concerned about it. I have my own routine so I am worried that we cannot get used to the new norm of him staying home.

I work three days a week in the office so he will be left alone at home during those days. On the other two days, I have my own exercise habits and social routines with my friends. Although he assures me that we will figure it out, I really want to have a realistic conversation about it.

I heard about how divorces happen when one party retires. I feel so worried that this may happen to us. I am fearful about sharing this thought with my husband. How can I approach this conversation so that it does not end with us quarrelling? I really want to make this work!

Thinking Differently

This is a big transition! Retirement is not about stopping work, but being able to not work for money. This is an amazing stage of life. He has worked so hard all his life, now is the time to celebrate and really focus on the things that he wants to do. It is a joyous event and it is a great time to invite gratitude into your lives.

I can see why you are concerned with regards to your different habits, schedules and needs. I also applaud your desire to have a frank and open conversation with your husband so that it will help to create a new lifestyle for the both of you. It can also be exciting with new possibilities, now that he has the time, resources and freedom to do so.

Moving Forward

1. Have an open conversation
This includes listening to your husband's hopes and dreams. It is very tempting to just jump into the list of things to do and plan for. How about talking about what is so exciting for him? What are this thoughts and feelings about this stage of his life? He will also have fears even if he does not show it or talk about it. How can you share in his major transition? Allow your husband to bask in his moment, but also remind him that both of you share a life together. So, share with him what you think, love and fear.

2. Have a plan together
After both of you have talked through your true feelings about his retirement and understood each other, this is the time to start planning your finances, daily life routines, needs and wants. Create a plan that includes exploration, travel and fun in your lives. Do not forget to include other loved ones, like family and friends, into your plan. After all, what is life without love?

3. Review your plan periodically
Agree upon a time frame that you will both review your collective plan on a regular basis. This will make sure

the two of you are each heard by the other party. It will also allow you to tweak your plans to make sure both needs and wants are met. Perhaps after a good rest, he may want to work again.

4. Set boundaries

While you live a shared life, you also must have your own time and space. Set boundaries to make sure that both of you respect the individual time you need for your hobbies and friends. This is, of course, making sure this individual time does not affect your life as a couple.

5. Be present

During the times together, be fully present for each other. Enjoy the meal or activity you are participating in together. As you move into this new stage of life, put your mind and attention into the new journey.

Reflection for Clarity

- How can I celebrate this life stage achievement with my husband?

- What is important to our identity as a couple?

- Who else is affected by this transition?

- What are our goals and our shared vision for the future?

- What will keep us going?

I Am Retiring

"Often when you think you're at the end of something, you're at the beginning of something else."
– Fred Rogers

Transition Story

For the last 40 years, I always thought of myself as an engineer. This has always been who I am and how I introduced myself. I am proud to be one. As long as I work, I can continue to call myself an engineer. Now that I am retiring, I am at a loss. I am not looking forward to the last day of work. My family is planning a big party for me, but I am not excited at all.

My husband is already looking to plan for our trip around the world. I should be happy, but I am dreading it. I have an ex-colleague who is disillusioned about retirement and feels bored and useless. I do not want to end up like that, but I do want to retire, spend time with my elderly parents and explore other interests.

What is happening to me? Is this conflicting bunch of feelings normal?

Thinking Differently

First and foremost, how you are feeling is more common than you know. Most people may not want to talk about difficult feelings and feel pressured to be happy about retirement by their loved ones. Great job in identifying and facing up to your difficult feelings!

Yes, traditionally, retirement is something to look forward to, but it is a huge change and transition in your life. This is especially so if you have loved your lifelong profession and it has become part of your identity. To retire feels like a detachment of that connection to your profession and in a way, cut off from that part of your life.

It does not have to be that way though. Retirement just means that you no longer have to work for money and you will have more freedom of time. This allows you to pursue other interests you have and contribute to your community in a different way. It can be one of the most fulfilling times of your life. You may even want to take up a job that inspires and interests you!

Moving Forward

1. Share your thoughts and feelings with someone you trust

It is important that you are able to talk through and express your thoughts and feelings about your impending retirement with someone. This will help you process your thoughts and emotions, and progress towards the journey ahead. Bottling them up inside may cause emotional outbursts that may result in more headaches.

2. Mentor aspiring young engineers

Find a way to mentor aspiring young engineers. Volunteer your time with your professional association or speak with the universities for an adjunct position to share your lifelong experience as an engineer. This will keep you connected to your profession and contribute to others by inspiring them.

3. Teach

The knowledge you have accumulated in the last 40 years is so valuable. Why not teach? Find a school or university which specialises in engineering and work with them to deliver a course that will help in improving the technical capabilities of young engineers. You can even work with your current workplace to do the same for their newly hired engineers.

4. Explore the kind of retirement life you want
The traditional view of retirement shows pictures of people playing golf or baking cakes. It does not have to be that way for you. Explore other parts of you that you may not have time to during your years of working. You can even work part-time as an engineer if it is a workable arrangement, leaving time to explore other passions.

5. Be open to exploring new things
Now that you have the time and space, why not try new things? Other than being an engineer, what other interests did you have when you were younger that you really enjoyed?

Reflection for Clarity

- What do I want to look forward to after retirement?

- Who do I want to become?

- How do I want to feel in creating this new stage of life?

- What is the most important thing to me now?

- What do I want to do that I could not when I worked full-time?

Work Life Changes

I Want to Return to Work After a Career Break

"Starting over is the opportunity to come back better than before."

– **Ryan Kahn**

Transition Story

When my kids were approaching puberty, I took a five-year career break to look after them. I made this decision because I wanted to be there for them when they were growing up. Now that they have all grown up and need less of me, I want to go back to the workforce.

Despite my best efforts, I am finding it difficult to return to the career arena. While searching for jobs that may be suitable for me, I have sent out numerous applications, but interviews have been scarce. This really discourages me.

In the few interviews that I did get invited to, the conversation would inevitably be focused on my career break instead of my rich experience and skillset. I feel frustrated about this and often become too conscious and stressed up over it. I would then end up not doing well during the interview. This insecurity is affecting the narrative of myself and my professional image. I really want to be confident and assured!

Perhaps I should not have taken the break! What should I do now?

Thinking Differently

What a noble decision you made for your life and your family by prioritising your kids' major transition of puberty! When you made the decision, you explored all options and came to this conclusion of taking a career break. It was an informed choice and whether it was voluntary or involuntary, it is not important.

What is important is that it was a worthy investment of time and attention on yourself and/or your family. Time was needed for you to do what you had to do. There is nothing to be ashamed of and there is no need to downplay this decision. It is part of the season of your life. Learn to accept it as it really is. Now you can start afresh and design your journey to be better than before!

Moving Forward

1. Be authentic

Speak about your career break with courage, authenticity and candour. There is no need to make up a story or sugar-coat the reality. This is important, as your posture, tone and attitude will shine through. For the employers, they need to know that you made an informed decision and is confident enough to speak about it. If asked, explain in a straightforward manner about the break.

2. Keep updated

Make sure you keep yourself updated on what's happening in your field. Things have changed during your break, but if you have not been upskilling yourself, it is not too late. Educate yourself on the latest happening in your field. There are many online courses, high quality blogs and formal classes that can bring you up to par with your industry standards. Even if you are choosing to change industry, you should do the same. Nothing is impossible if you put your mind to it.

3. Tap on your network

Make sure you keep in contact with your network, including co-workers, friends and industry contacts. Reach out to them to meet for coffee or lunch. Attend appropriate networking events that would be helpful for you to both update your knowledge and grow your network. You can also reach out to a recruiter or two to understand what is needed in the role that you desire. You will never know who in your network might help you get your next job.

4. Update your résumé and interview skills

If you have not updated your résumé for a while, this is the time to do so. It is the first calling card that you send to a potential employer. Make sure you have information that is clear, succinct and relevant in your résumé. Hire a career coach to help you through the details in writing an eye-catching résumé if you are not sure. Online presence is important today so make sure you have an updated LinkedIn profile if you have not already done so. Many companies and recruiters look for suitable candidates using online platforms.

Résumé aside, it is also important to update yourself on good interviewing skills. What to wear, how to present yourself and how to speak confidently are all important aspects of performing well in an interview. Role play with a friend/coach to help you practice what to say and how to say it.

5. Do not give up

Attitude is everything. If you walk into an interview desperate to get the job, it will show up in your posture, energy and the way you speak. It is important that you be patient with yourself and keep your spirits up. This will enable you to approach the job search with more positivity and thus, the ability to keep to the path on finding your ideal career.

Make sure that you take good care of yourself during this time. Eat well, have enough sleep and exercise. This will help to manage your emotional health and help you to appreciate everything that you have right now.

Reflection for Clarity

- What does returning to work mean to me?

- What do I want to be grateful for?

- Who would I like to become in the future?

- How can I contribute to my growth?

- How can I help others?

I Want to Quit My Job

"Your job is not just to do what your parents say, what your teachers say, what society says, but to figure out what your heart calling is and to be led by that."

– **Oprah Winfrey**

Transition Story

I have been wanting to quit my job for some time now. When I shared this desire with my best friends and family, they immediately jumped and said how good my current job is and that I should not leave it. In fact, one friend even asked me if I have lost my mind!

I still want to work in this industry, but I want a change in scenery and work in a different part of it. There is no horrible boss or particularly tough challenge that I am facing. I am so surprised that everyone around me is not at all supportive. I have spent a decade in the same job in the same company. I am bored and I am curious what it is like in other parts of the industry. Yes, I have heard stories and have had experiences shared with me. Surely it is nothing like if I were to experience it first-hand?

How can I make that change? With all the discouragements I am getting, I am also struggling with feelings of doubt.

Thinking Differently

Change is hard and uncomfortable, even the ones we want. When you change, the people around you will also need to change. They also struggle with this discomfort. As humans, we are wired to like stability so any change, no matter how small, can be like a pebble in our shoe.

Did your loved ones share their feelings—not thoughts or opinions—on this matter? Are they worried about you, alarmed because this is not like you? Perhaps they are also struggling and wondering what it means to them and what they need to change.

However, I applaud your efforts in thinking through this change and why you want it. Your desire to explore your curiosity and increase your learning is to be celebrated. There is nothing wrong in wanting a change and having different experiences.

Moving Forward

1. Be really clear that this is what you want
Make sure you do the deep work with yourself to make sure this is really what you want. Boredom may be the trigger, but what deeper reasons do you feel compel you to want to make this change? If you are shaken by what others think, then is this really what you want? If you think you cannot figure this out yourself, work with a trusted coach or mentor who can help you from a neutral perspective.

2. Share your feelings
Instead of trying to persuade your loved ones, help them to understand how you feel about the transition you want to move into. It is not about sharing your thoughts or arguments, but how you feel now and what you want to feel in moving into a new environment. This will show them your perspective and help you to frame that narrative for yourself.

3. Show them that you have thought it through
Share your thought process so your loved ones can understand that you have thought it through. This is because they are important to you and you need their support and encouragement. You do not need their

agreement—you only seek their understanding that you have thought through, want and need this change in your life for your personal growth.

4. Ask directly for support

Ask your loved ones for their support and encouragement directly. Even if they disagree with the decision, they can still help you with your transition. Ask for what you need from them in clear terms.

5. Speak to others in your field

Contact your peers in your field who work for other similar companies. This is a good time to find out from them the similarities, differences, opportunities and landscape from their points of view. This way, you can get current information and data that will help you understand the new area of interest with clarity before you make the shift. This will also help you to position yourself better and articulate better with regards to your desire to make a change.

6. Don't quit until...

You have done your homework and really know what you are getting yourself into with the change. Your feelings may be overwhelming at times so breathe and recentre yourself. Get all the pre-work done, create a transition plan and only execute the action when you are ready. You do not have to rush this.

Reflection for Clarity

- What do I want with this change?

- Who are the people in my life who can support me?

- What happens if I do not change?

- What are my values and strengths?

- What is my vision for my life?

I Want to Take a Career Break

"Rest is not idleness and to lie sometimes on the grass under trees on a summer's day, listening to the murmur of the water, or watching the clouds float across the sky, is by no means a waste of time."

– **John Lubbock**

Transition Story

I want to take a career break and have been talking to my husband about it. I am no longer feeling inspired in the work I do and I have no desire to continue working in a regular job. I feel burnt out and tired, and want to take a break to rest, to recuperate and to rejuvenate. I tried taking a vacation, but the moment I return to work, it is as if I never took a break.

I met with all kinds of resistance from friends and family members who were shocked that I would make such an “irresponsible” decision since I have young kids and aged parents to support. I know they were responding to this from their own deep fear of uncertainty. While I was sure at the beginning, their worry is starting to brush off me. I am frustrated and I do not know what to do. It is like getting lost in the jungle in a fog—the future is not clear and I do not know which way to go.

Thinking Differently

What a precious decision to put yourself first and know that you need to take a serious break and rest. We have been conditioned by our family and society to put others first and so we work hard to provide for our loved ones, many times disregarding our own needs. It is the courageous and brave who dares to see things for what they are and take the action to get what they need.

Moving Forward

1. Know the reasons

It sounds like you know exactly why you want this career break. You know you have to take a break or you will have a burnout. Be clear about your reasons for taking a breather from work. In fact, write it down and make sure you resonate with every reason. Whenever doubt casts its shadow on you, go back to this list and tap on the courage to make a change. Once you are in the career break, it will also serve to remind you why you made this transition.

2. Have a plan
Once you have your "why", even if the road is unclear, the fog will start to lift. Take a personal retreat and lay out your plans dilligently. Go down to the details of how long you will break for, what would you do during this time of rest, whose support do you need, etc. Be clear on how you want your break to look like and the goals and vision of what you want at the end of the break. It is an exercise of reality. It does not matter if you do not do these things or life happens and plans change. The important thing is that you have a direction.

3. Speak to others who have taken a career break
Find others—it could be a friend or co-worker—who have taken a career break and gather their thoughts and advice. It will show you how it is possible to take a career break. It will help you see the possible obstacles and also ways to overcome them. Knowing the reality of taking a career break will help prepare you better for what is to come.

4. Get help
As much as our loved ones care for us, sometimes what you need is a different perspective from objective

professionals. Getting help from a counsellor for difficult emotional struggles will solidify your plan and your resolve to make this change for yourself. This can be a mentor who has walked the path or a coach who can help you get clarity.

5. Make the decision bravely

Once you have everything you need, make the decision. Knowing the purpose of your break is a powerful energy that will keep you going, even when faced with objections and obstacles.

Reflection for Clarity

- What do I hope to get out of this break?

- Who are the people in my life who can support me?

- What happens if I do not rest?

- What positive intentions will this break bring for me?

- How important is this decision for my well-being?

I Got Laid Off/ Retrenched

"You cannot control what happens to you,
but you can control your attitude towards what happens
to you, and in that, you will be mastering change
rather than allowing it to master you."
– **Brian Tracy**

Transition Story

I went to work one day and found my security pass not working while scanning myself into my office. When I checked in with the receptionist, I was told to wait. The next thing I knew, I was given a box of my personal belongings and a letter informing me that I was retrenched. I was in shock and disbelief as I stood there with the box and letter in my hands. I felt hurt, angry and abandoned. I even worked late the night before to complete a project.

I kept thinking if there were signs that I had missed. There was no warning whatsoever and my manager never even had a conversation with me at all. While the company has given me a decent severance package, I am completely devastated and shocked. I am questioning my performance, my value as a person and my work as a professional.

I feel stuck and at a loss of what to do.

Thinking Differently

This is one of the most difficult transitions in life, especially when no prior warning or conversation was given. Your feelings are completely normal as you enter this unplanned transition. Even as this has happened, you must remember that your performance, value as a person and as a professional is more than just work.

Your life consists of many areas and facets, and your worth is not just based on your work. You have more than one identity and you must not let this bump on your life journey trip you up. You are valuable, loved and cared for.

Moving Forward

1. Take the time
Allow yourself time to breathe, calm down and get clear-headed. This may take a while so do not rush it. As you were rushed into an abrupt ending, you must take charge and give yourself permission to process everything, every feeling, every thought, every action. Do not think about what to do yet nor take action of any kind. At this moment, self-care and self-compassion must be your top priority.

2. Seek support
Reach out to your support network, be it your family, friends and even former co-workers. Enlist their help and support to work through the enormous emotional upheaval and sudden change in your life. If the feelings are too powerful, get professional help from psychiatrists, psychologists and/or counsellors. They are trained to help you through this. There is no shame in asking for help—only the strongest people ask for help. Do the same for your family who may also be impacted from your loss, but focus on yourself first. You do not have to do this alone.

3. Get clear
A transition is one of the times that one can get clarity about one's vision, future and what one wants going forward. You may want to return to a similar position you left and stay within the same industry or you

may want to explore different industries and different interests. The main thing is to get the clarity you need to formulate a plan. One of the most powerful tools is reflection and journaling. By writing down what you want and how you want to feel in your future, you are moving towards clarity of your goals.

4. Move your body and eat well
Physical exercise is one of the best ways to get your mood up. When you move your body, endorphins are released and these feel good hormones can help you pick yourself up naturally. Filling yourself with healthy and wholesome food will build your resistance against mental health issues and help you to sleep better at night. Take care of yourself this way so that you can get the clarity you need to move forward.

5. Formulate a plan
When you are able to, sit down for a day or two to put together a plan that you can build your future life on. Remember that this is only a transition. The painful ending can pave the way for a new beginning. How will you use this experience to help yourself move ahead? How will you use this experience to help others who may be going through this as well? Think of this as an opportunity to reset your professional life.

Reflection for Clarity

- What do I want in my life?

- I know I can be fulfilled again. What will I do to achieve it?

- Who can help me with this plan?

- What are my obstacles and how can I overcome them?

- What am I grateful for?

I Have a New Job

"Take the first step in faith.
You don't have to see the whole staircase,
just take the first step."
– **Martin Luther King Jr.**

Transition Story

I am in a new job for about three months now. The work is quite fulfilling, but I am struggling to fit into the team. I am at least seven or eight years older than my teammates. While we can work well together, I feel like I am being left out of social events and I do not understand a lot of the new lingo they use. They go bar hopping and don't return home until wee hours of the day. I have a family so other than the occasional team dinner, I cannot and have no desire to participate in their outings. I have spoken to my team leader, but he is unconcerned.

Recently, I think my colleagues are gossiping about me behind my back, saying that I am old and inflexible. This was due to an incident where I had to put my foot down on the project requirements. Other than feeling not part of the team, I am now also ostracised due to my professional opinion. I am really hurt by their reaction.

What can I do to connect with them better?

Thinking Differently

It is great that you are coming from a position of wanting to connect with your colleagues better. Indeed, when a team is made up of members from different age groups, generations and backgrounds, it can cause friction due to the different ways of working and thinking. However, knowing and accepting that this is bound to happen is the first step towards finding better ways to connect with each other.

With your experience, you add value to the team and the company in a way that is different from them. Helping them see that instead of thinking you are lording over them would help them to leverage your experience at work.

Moving Forward

1. Accept the difference

Before they can see and accept the difference between you and them, you must do the same. When you leverage their young minds in getting new ideas and leverage your experience in navigating work obstacles, there is a new cooperation that can benefit the performance of the team. Accept that you have different interests and priorities from them and that is okay.

2. Be curious

Ask questions first to understand their point of view. Instead of judging them, use your curiosity to explore their way of thinking. Phrase your questions in an open and non-judgemental way and truly listen to understand. They will appreciate your effort, maybe not at first, but over time, it will reach out to them.

3. Talk to them one on one

Find a chance to connect with your young co-workers one on one. Most times, this will take away the group dynamics and allow you to help them understand you as well. This may be hard in the beginning and you may get rejected. Start with small talks at the pantry before striking up the courage to get lunch together.

4. Go with their decisions

When it is relevant and there is no difference either way, go with their decision and thinking. Allow them to see that you are not here to dictate how things are done. You are here to work with them and achieve the best results together. There is no individual credit, only team performance. Be the leader that you are.

5. Learn how to communicate collaboratively
While you do not need to be the best of friends to work well together, it is important that you communicate in a way that says you are equals. Working to understand them and helping them understand you, your communication style can be flexible and adjusted to their style to bridge the understanding. This is a continuous journey and it will take time and commitment for this to happen. Be patient with yourself and with them.

Reflection for Clarity

- How do I want this relationship to look like?

- What do I need to let go for this to move forward?

- What can I do to learn the skills I need?

- Who in the organisation can help mentor me?

- How can we be successful as a team?

I Have a New Manager

"The real winners in life are the people who look at every situation with an expectation that they can make it work or make it better."
– **Barbara Pletcher**

Transition Story

I worked very well with my manager, so when I was told she was leaving and I will have a new manager, I felt sad and anxious. This is because I have a great relationship with my manager and I am not sure how it is going to be with her replacement.

When the new manager came, he was introduced to the team. He seemed okay at first, however, as time went by, I found a lot of difficulties in working with him. He does not give clear instructions and I was often unable to see where we are going. When I asked him repeatedly, he will wave me away and say that I should just focus on the one thing he asked me to do. It is demeaning as I have been working in my role for the last eight years.

I am angry and frustrated all the time and it is affecting my professional judgement and my performance at work. While unhappy with my new situation, I do not want to leave the company as I really love the work I do and the people there.

What can I do to overcome this situation?

Thinking Differently

In this situation, you are going through two transitions: The first is your ex-manager's departure and the second is your new manager's entry into your work life. As they happened one after another, there may be overlaps that you are still processing. When you compare the two managers who have different styles, inevitably, the transitions become hard.

Remember that you cannot control others. You can only control yourself, your thoughts, your emotions, your actions. With this unfamiliar and perhaps at times stressful environment, your survival instincts are being triggered and fear may be the underlying emotion. It is important to notice that and be aware that you are being triggered by a different working style.

When that happens, it is wired in you to behave in a way to protect and defend yourself. Observe that and confirm whether or not you really are in danger. In this case, it may be just a simple case of different working styles. If so, focusing on fostering understanding between each other may be the key to making the working environment more suitable for you.

Moving Forward

1. Accept the new reality
If you have not let go of the lovely working experience with your ex-boss, this is the time. Keep it as a great experience and memory, but do not compare your two bosses. It is hard not to, but remember that not letting go and not accepting the new reality will stop you from moving forward. They are different people so rather than live in the past, move on in the present.

2. Think about your career goal
What is your career goal in this company? If you have a path you want to follow and this is slowing you down, ask yourself what you can do to move pass this obstacle. This reflection is very important so take the time away from work and spend a few hours in a location that is relaxing for you to journal about your

vision of your career. Writing and articulating what you need will give you the clarity you want.

3. Put yourself in his shoes

Ask yourself why he is doing this and what is his style of working. Is it true that he is a very difficult person to work with or that his attitude is not what you think is right? Think through his lens and see if you can find anything else that may be a new insight. For this, try your best to remove your lens and put on a neutral one.

4. Ask for support

There may be others who are working with him or have worked with him. If things are working for them, then figure out how you can work with him and what you can ask from him to help you. If things are not working for them, learn about their experiences and how they have dealt with it.

5. Have a plan

After you have done all you can to figure out how to work with him and you have new insights about this, but still think this partnership will not work, then it is time to think about what your next steps can be. You can do it yourself by journaling, working with a coach or finding a trusted friend to bounce off ideas on what you can and want to do. Even if you decide to stay, know that you made a conscious decision to do so.

This will help you to tap into your resilience and move through this with more grace and acceptance.

Reflection for Clarity

- What do I really what from this relationship?

- Do I still want this relationship in my life?

- What can I ask for that would help me?

- How can I reframe this so that it will serve me and my growth?

- What thoughts and emotions do I have that are not moving me forward?

I Got Promoted

"People don't get promoted for doing their jobs really well. They get promoted by demonstrating their potential to do more."
– **Tara Jaye Frank**

Transition Story

I was extremely successful as a sales executive in my firm and consistently hit all my financial targets. After two years of working very hard, I finally got promoted to sales leader. I now manage a team of six sales executives.

Two months in, I realised that I am doing very little sales work. I do not see my clients anymore and I really miss that. The six team members have various challenges and my main job now is to make them highly effective and successful sales executives.

I do not know how to manage a team and I often feel anxious walking into team meetings. I do not have the skills to manage and coach them, and my own bosses are impatient for results. They want me to deliver the same stellar results I used to.

I am too embarrassed to ask for my old job back, which is what I really enjoy. What should I do?

Thinking Differently

For starters, take the time to acknowledge your authenticity and vulnerability in recognising this! The first step to thinking differently is to be honest and clear about what is really happening. The first thing to be clear about is if you really want your old job back or do you want to take up the challenge to learn to be a team leader? What values do you profess and what are your strengths? Reflect about what you want to be known for in the workplace. Once you are clear, the next steps will also become clearer and simpler.

Keep in mind that you were promoted because you performed well. This is a good thing as you are being recognised and acknowledged. Therefore, do not take that away from yourself. Moving into a different role is a transition—it is unfamiliar and you are working hard to make sense of it, on top of your new responsibilities.

Moving Forward

1. Get clarity
Make sure that you really explore that feeling of anxiety and not knowing what to do. Most people do not like to move out of their comfort zone and explore new things. Be clear whether this is the reason or is it true that your previous role is what you really want and not because of the discomfort of the new responsibilities.

2. Speak to a mentor
Get access to a mentor who has walked the path you are on. This person can be in the same company or can be someone in a professional organisation you belong to. Ask him or her the hard questions and why he or she made the choice he or she made. Find out if he or she has valuable resources that can help you to forward your thinking.

3. Ask for a coach
Be honest with your manager about what is happening once you are clear. It is important that you trust that your leaders are supportive of your development. Ask to have a coach in helping you with either moving back to your old role or adjusting to the new one. This is very common in the corporate world and your

coach will journey alongside you and help you to think through how to navigate this new path.

4. Make a choice

If you have done everything you humanly can to work on this and you find that this is still not the path for you, then make a choice. You have to have the courage to choose the path that makes you most happy. Speak to trusted leaders in your organisation to ease back into the work that you are best at and is most aligned with who you are.

5. Move forward

No matter what choice you made after clarifying what you want, be at peace. Move forward with pride and optimism into the path of your choice. It is important that you continue to see this as a success in your career.

Reflection for Clarity

- What is important to me about this job?

- How would embarrassment and guilt serve me?

- What do I want to be proud of in my work?

- Who do I want to become?

- What am I willing to do to be happy?

I No Longer Enjoy My Work

"Our first half is about how to make a living and our second half has the promise of being about how to make a life."

– **Bob Buford**

Transition Story

When I first started working in the company 15 years ago, it was new and exciting. There were always new things to learn and I really enjoyed connecting with my co-workers and clients around the world. Business travel was something I looked forward to because I was able to travel the world and broaden my horizons. Even after 10 years, the work was fulfilling and I could see how I am contributing to my industry and my team. The leaders were visionary, the managers were supportive and my co-workers were collaborative. I became a manager of a small team of five.

In my 12th year, I started to notice that I was no longer positive about my work. I criticised the clients, did not support my team as I would have done in the past and I dreaded going back to work after the weekends. I was so confused as I have never felt like this before. It is as if I do not fit in anymore—or should I say that work no longer have a place in my life.

I have been hanging on for a year now and I am completely miserable. I am really scared. I thought I was going to be here until I retire.

What is happening to me?

Thinking Differently

There comes a time in our lives when we shift gears and move into a time of meaning rather than just achievements. Through the years, you have built a great and lovely life for yourself. Celebrate that growth and opportunities! It is indeed very confusing as you are in an unfamiliar territory of a life transition. Your inside has changed and your outside is no longer aligned with what has changed.

This is a great opportunity! You now can recreate a life of meaning, dreams and joy for yourself. While that can be scary, it can also be fulfilling, rich and fun! If you take the first courageous step, it will be a brave new world.

Moving Forward

1. Assess the situation

Talk to co-workers and mentors you trust to check in and get outside perspective on how you are doing. It is important to have different views to your work and how you are looking at it. Was there a big change in the company or was there a particular setback that really affected you? Speak to your family and friends to get a pulse check on your behaviour, thoughts and feelings outside of work to get a complete picture.

2. Seek professional help

If you realise it is something that needs professional help from counsellors, psychologists or coaches, do not hesitate to engage them. These are trained professionals who can help you accelerate your thinking, processing and paving your way forward.

3. Create an action plan

Once you know what is the root of the issue, create an action plan. It would be even better if you have three to five trusted people in your life who can support you in your action plan creation. They can suggest ideas, support your thoughts and assist you in carrying them out. They can also be the buffer to naysayers, should you choose to go a different route.

4. Experiment

It is scary to make major changes in your life. Experimenting is the best way to gain more perspective. This will help you to know if something you like in your head is something you like in real life. It will give you more information and thus help you to tweak your plan to something more appropriate. Take your time to experiment.

5. Take the plunge

After you are done experimenting, take the next step with courage. Some things take time to gain traction or see results. Be brave and lean on those who will support, encourage and celebrate with you. Your persistence will be rewarded.

Reflection for Clarity

- Who do I want to be?

- What do I want to be known for?

- What will light my fire and create meaning for me?

- What do I want to leave behind?

- What do I enjoy?

I Want to Pursue a New Field of Work

"The first step towards getting somewhere is to decide you're not going to stay where you are."

– J. P. Morgan

Transition Story

I have been a corporate marketing professional all my working life. I am good at what I do and have enjoyed much success in marketing. In the last few years, marketing has gone online and I had to learn new skills and perspectives. Increasingly, I am unable to connect as well with the customer base that I am accustomed to. It has been frustrating professionally and I noticed myself distancing and disengaging from my work.

Recently, I have taken on a new hobby of baking sourdough bread. The process of baking is so mindful and calming. It is amazing to be able to create something out of simple ingredients. I am always eager and excited to try new recipes and as it turns out, I am really good at it. I really love it and have received wonderful compliments from my friends and family. One of my nieces loved it so much that she wanted to create an Instagram account for me so that I can sell my bread. I am seriously considering doing it full-time!

Have I lost my mind? How do I know I am making the right decision?

Thinking Differently

What a wonderful discovery about yourself! It is obvious you really enjoy baking sourdough bread and sharing it. Most have us have talents and skills that are never explored. It sounds like the alternative path was never considered and perhaps considered unconventional and uncertain.

Instead of asking yourself why, you should ask yourself why not. This will give you some headway into thinking how you can design your life in a way that leverages your strength and gives you joy.

Moving Forward

1. Reflect on your current state

Think about what is really happening in your profession. Is it something you can continue to stay on in or is it a definite no? Give yourself time and not rush into making any major decision. This is to ensure that all decisions will be made knowingly, with a plan and knowing all the risks.

2. Explore your options

Do you really need to quit to bake? Work hard to gain clarity as to what works. Explore and find out what other options are there instead of zooming in on only one alternative. Discuss your options with people you trust and tap on their wisdom and experience.

3. Know your gains and losses

Create a list of gains and losses against all your options. Be clear and honest with yourself. This is to ensure that you know exactly what you are gaining and losing, no matter which decision you make. Do the research for every option to make sure you understand thoroughly, even if it is a decision you may not like.

4. Talk to mentors

Seek and find mentors who have made this change and switched to another line of work. Talk to them, have them share their experiences and learn from the mistakes they have made. Make it real for yourself.

5. Decide

Make a decision and stick with it. Take the time to go through the process of becoming a professional in your chosen second line of work or start learning new skills in the profession you love. Give it your all and gain the joy you want.

Reflection for Clarity

- What do I want from this change?

- Who can support me in this change?

- What do I need to know to make this change?

- How do I want to feel?

- How will this change the way my life looks like?

Personal Changes

My Parent Passed Away

"All the art of living lies in a fine mingling of letting go and holding on."
– **Havelock Ellis**

Transition Story

My heart filled with dread as the doctor told me my mother only had six months to live. It was a truly surreal conversation as I pondered the imminent death of my mother and honestly, I could not really hear what the doctor was saying.

I felt suspended in time when he told me to take her home and engage palliative care. There was nothing more they can do for her at the hospital. Two weeks ago, she passed away in our family home.

The most painful time was not just after she passed. In fact, I was so busy sorting out the funeral and administrative procedures, I do not even have time to think and merely proceeded to do the next thing in front of me. When everything was over and I had to pack her belongings to throw or donate, that was when it really hit me. Every piece of clothing, paper and jewellery has a story and I struggled to make the decisions. I would run to the bathroom in the middle of the workday to cry in the cubicle. I miss her.

I know this will pass and I will survive. I just do not know how I can help myself through this.

Thinking Differently

Knowing this will pass is a good start to the grieving process. Everyone handles loss and grief differently and there is no one way to do it. It is also important that you understand that grief is an important process, a transition, in searching for a different life without your mother. Research has shown that most people can recover from loss on their own through the passing of time if they have social support and healthy habits. In some cases, they may need support from mental healthcare professionals.

There is no standard timeframe for moving through grief. Take the time you need to celebrate your mother's life and adjust to a life without her.

Moving Forward

1. Honour and remember

You can do this by talking about her to others in your life, like other family members, friends and co-workers. This is one of the ways to get social support and connection, and will help you to move through the grieving process with more ease and peace.

2. Accept your feelings

Know that feelings will come and go, and you will experience a wide spectrum of feelings ranging from sadness to anger to weariness. Treat your feelings as guests coming into your house. Sit with them and accept that they will leave when their time is up.

3. Live your life

Live your life as normally as you can muster. Keep to your routines and even when grief or triggers descend, acknowledge them and do your best to move through them. Allow yourself to take the time to pause in your daily life to handle them.

4. Self-care

Healthy habits of self-care are very important when you are moving through grief. Grief is essentially trauma to your system and to heal, you have to make sure you take good care of yourself. This means eating well, doing physical exercises, sleeping well, going outside, spending time with friends and family, reading, listening to music, making art or anything else that would help you feel recharged and refreshed.

5. Spend time with loved ones

Allow your loved ones to help you through your grief. If they are grieving like you, support each other. Spend time together talking, doing activities that you all enjoy and giving yourselves a reason to get out of bed.

6. Get help

If you are unable to handle the grief and has prolonged signs of depression, seek help from mental health professionals. They are trained to help you move through the difficult terrain of grief. Remember that only the strong asks for help so get all the help you need.

Reflection for Clarity

- What do I want to remember about her?

- How can I move through grief with peace?

- In what ways can I celebrate her life?

- How would I like to be in this new life?

- What can I look forward to?

I Moved to a New Country

"The art of life is a constant readjustment to our surroundings."
– **Kakuzo Okakaura**

Transition Story

I just moved to Singapore from the US. I had followed my husband on his overseas assignment to lead a team of 100 people here. While it was an exciting opportunity, I relocated with a lot of uncertainties and worry in my heart.

As I left without a job, I focused on getting us settled here in our new home in a new country. My kids have all settled down in their new school with their new friends. I try to keep it simple day to day as I work through the culture shock and the feeling of missing my family and friends back home.

Now that I have some time and space to think, I have been struggling to find the work I like. I was a professional marketer in the US and I find difficulty in finding this type of work here in Singapore. I truly am at a loss in this foreign country as I struggle to adjust.

Although I have a few friends from the American Club, I do not know how I can fill my time.

Thinking Differently

Congratulations on a new adventure in Asia! What an exciting time and a great opportunity to reset what you can do. You have done all you can to move and stabilise your family. Now it is your time to design the life that you desire.

Many skills in your professional life can be transferred or repurposed. Often, you can explore and experiment using your skills in different settings. Some of the ways you can embark on it is to start volunteering, attend networking events and speak to professional recruiters. These will afford you the perspectives of others and help you to see things more broadly than what you alone can see in a new country.

It is also important to give yourself room to adjust and transit to a new country. Practice self-compassion and be patient with yourself. Celebrate every small success and over time, you will find your place here.

Moving Forward

1. Take the time
You are in a completely new environment and culture. Take the time to explore and understand this change. Learn to appreciate the new ways of living, doing and being, and see what works for you. Slow down and take in everything that is fresh and exciting. This will help you to assimilate and be comfortable.

2. Keep the connection
It is important to maintain your connection with those back home in the US. This will keep you grounded and get the support you need for this transition. Remember to leverage the wonderful technology that we have. Keeping in touch with what is happening back home will help ease your transition back home in future.

3. Accept the differences
Indeed, everything seems different. Perhaps even the water tastes different! It may take a while to move to acceptance so start with appreciating the goodness of your host country. By being grateful for the good things afforded to you in this new environment, it will

allow you to have experiences that may not be possible back home.

4. Have realistic expectations

The job market may be very different and roles offered may not be a perfect fit to what you are good at. Having realistic expectations in your search for a job that inspires you may take a while and lots of conversations! Be proactive in finding out about the offering and ask lots of questions to help you know how to position yourself.

5. Make new friends

Challenge yourself to move outside of your comfort zone and make new friends! Do not limit yourself to people whom you are comfortable with or people like you. You will never know when you will meet a friend for life.

Reflection for Clarity

- What are my personal values?

- What do others see me do well in?

- What sets my soul on fire?

- What would I do without getting paid?

- How would I like to think about this new chapter of my life?

I Lost My Best Friend

"New beginnings are often disguised as painful endings."

– **Lao Tzu**

Transition Story

I knew my best friend since we were 12 years old. We were schoolmates and happen to attend the same after school care centre. We grew up close and confided in each other as we journeyed through our difficult teenage years.

When we started dating, we were each other's shoulder to cry on when things did not go well. We shared everything. College came and went. We joined the workforce and still met for meals and drinks. Slowly, as time went by, our meetings became few and far in between. While we were so happy when the other got married, things started to change even more as we started to get busy with our own families.

During one recent dinner which I arranged, we talked about our lives, our perspectives and our dreams. Once close, I realised that night that we have taken very different paths and have very different values. Although we are still friends, she is no longer my best friend. We have so many opposing views and while we kept it civil, I knew in my heart that we lost that intimate friendship a long time ago.

I cried that night and I wonder how I can ever get over this.

Thinking Differently

There are seasons in life and during these different seasons, different people come and go. While your friend was close to you when you were growing up, in this season, she is not meant to stay. This does not mean that you have lost her forever, for nothing in life stays permanent. There are those of us who are completely different, but stayed as lifelong friends. They may not be very close at certain times of their lives, but during a crisis, they lean on each other.

Your friend is still very much a part of your history and life. While things may have changed, this does not mean that you need to let go of this friendship.

Moving Forward

1. Take the initiative

If you do want your relationship to be closer, then take the initiative to know this friend as if she is a new friend. Be curious and explorative as to who she is, what views she holds and why she holds them. You will never know what you will find, which may be the very thing you never considered to be a binding factor between you two.

2. Accept the present

Accept that she is now different and that she has to accept the current you as well. Perhaps she is feeling the same as you. Open up a conversation and talk about your differences and celebrate your similarities.

3. Have new experiences together

Just like corporate teams do team building, do something fun together that you have not done before. Try out the latest virtual reality experience, explore a new park or try a new cuisine for instance. This will give you fresh experiences to build your relationship on.

4. Continue to love her

Continue your friendship, love and concern for her. Life goes in cycles and relationships have their ups and downs. While you traverse through the downs, remember that it can still go up for the both of you.

5. Have a conversation

You can share your thoughts and feelings with her about this. Let her know how you see your relationship and how important she is in your life. Find a way to reach an understanding that you can still be best friends despite having different views.

Reflection for Clarity

- Why is this friendship so important to me?

- What can I do to reframe this relationship and see it in a new light?

- How can I develop a new intimacy between us?

- How can I let go of my expectations?

- What would I like to invite into this relationship?

I Fell Sick

"You can't start the next chapter if you keep re-reading the last one."

– **Unknown**

Transition Story

I have always been a relatively healthy person. Having a healthcare training background, I eat well, exercise regularly and have a generally active life. I am fairly on top of my physical well-being and do annual health screenings. When my doctor looked worried at my latest test results and asked me to see a specialist, I was nonchalant about it.

When the specialist told me that I have stage 2 breast cancer, I was in disbelief for days. My mother was adopted and since she does not have breast cancer, she did not know if it runs in the family.

Thus began the days of chemotherapy and countless blood tests. I struggled daily with the physical challenges of the side effects of the treatments and I also felt frustrated and angry that this has happened to me. My life is upended and I am now a burden to my family as I need their support and help to battle this illness. I may even have to quit my job as the pace is quite punishing.

This is not how I envisioned my life to be. Why is this happening to me?

Thinking Differently

No one could have predicted what would happen in their lives. In addition, this is not something you could have known even if you know your genetic makeup. While you cannot change the reality of it, you can reframe how you see your life. Focus on what is important to you and take it one day at a time. Find a way to see this as an unexpected turn of events, but make the decision and take the time to move to acceptance so you can move pass this life challenge towards hope.

Moving Forward

1. Be future-focused

Do not focus on what could have been, but what can be. If you keep focusing on your loss and lament about what could have been, it will prevent you from experiencing what is happening in the present. Take it one step at a time and move towards a new life in the future.

2. Ask for help

Ask for help from your family and close ones, and lean on them as you will need the support in this journey of healing. Do not be embarrassed to ask. You need your community to rally around you as you confront cancer, even if it is just for a drink of water or a hug. Think about how you can help when you get better.

3. Seek relevant professionals

Just as you see an oncologist for the treatment of the breast cancer, remember to see a psychologist if you find the ordeal mentally too much to bear. You are human and there is no shame is seeking appropriate professional help. You do not need to know everything, just who to reach out to when you are unwell.

4. Acceptance as part of your life

Cancer is now a part of your life, whether you like it or not. If you are able to accept it as part of your life journey and your identity, you can then live with it and move past it. Make peace with this, but know that it does not define who you are.

5. Join support groups

There are many support groups out there that are made up of people with similar health challenges. Joining one can help you see things differently, pick up a few tips to improve your life and most importantly, have a group of people who understands and supports you.

Reflection for Clarity

- What do I need in order for me to confront this life challenge?

- What is the most meaningful way to live with cancer?

- Who can support me in redesigning my life after surviving cancer?

- How can I view this challenge positively?

- Who do I want to be?

I Am Divorced

"And so rock bottom became the solid foundation on which I rebuilt my life."

– J. K. Rowling

Transition Story

I am a single mother with two young kids, aged 4 and 6 years old. My ex-husband cheated on me and our divorce was finalised last week.

Throughout the whole proceedings, I was very focused on my kids and the legal process of divorce. While dealing with my own sense of betrayal, sadness and disappointment, I was simultaneously trying to find a place for us to live, figuring out the finances and working full-time. I could not work through the feelings and had to suppress them. Now that everything is sorted out, I am left with a gapping emptiness and all the feelings are now resurfacing in a big way.

I had a very different vision of how it was going to be. I never expected things to go so bad so fast. I am still spinning from the ordeal. I am at a loss of how my future will look like as a single mother struggling to raise my kids.

Thinking Differently

You have just gone through a particularly hard transition. You were just pushed through by the waves of change. There was no time to reflect and see what was happening to you on the inside.

Now that you have time to do it, take the time to do so. Even if it is painful, difficult and at times devastating, you must process everything that you have gone through. If you do not, it will always hold you back. Now that your outside is a clean slate, your inside has to catch up. Only then can you feel whole again.

Moving Forward

1. See a psychologist or counsellor

If you experience intense and difficult feelings or are not able to function well on a day to day basis, if you cannot help but think of the past, please seek the help of a mental health professional, such as a psychologist or counsellor. They will help you to work through the difficult feelings of loss and pain. It is the strong who asks for help so do not hesitate to do so.

2. Practice extreme self-care

Through the ordeal, you have put your children, security and stability first. Now that all that is sorted, take baby steps to include self-care activities in your schedule. Just as how the airlines always tell its passengers to put on their own air masks before helping others, you must first take care of yourself before you can take care of others. This includes having a healthy lifestyle of sleep, diet and exercise, surrounding yourself with people who love and support you, and participating in activities that you enjoy and which nurture you.

3. Take your time

There is no hurry, so slow down now that you are processing everything that has happened. Be compassionate and gentle with yourself. It is of utmost importance to take all the time you need.

4. Map out your future

If you do not know where to start, start by looking at the following three months. What would you like it to look like? What are your goals? Start small so that it is not overwhelming. When you feel up to it, you can then go on to look at longer stretches of time.

5. Find your tribe

Check out support groups or communities, whether secular or from religious organisations, which is specially targeted at single parents. This will help you to be among people who have similar experiences and values in journeying through your life as a single parent. You can ask questions or get help in dealing with difficult feelings.

Reflection for Clarity

- What do I want my life to mean?

- Who am I and who do I want to be?

- What help do I need to get past this?

- Who can I ask for help from?

- What can I let go?

Afterword

"Celebrate endings—for they precede new beginnings."
– Jonathan Lockwood Huie

I think about death at least once a day.

My own death, my loved ones' deaths and that of those who have passed on. I also think about the death of the spirit and the soul. It is the most sobering topic to think about for me. It helps me to come back to what is important and what is valuable in this lifetime. It is the fastest way to come back to the present. When things are not going well, I think more about death.

I am grateful every morning when I wake up for God has given me another day to live. I say that sometimes to myself and send a prayer of thanks up to Him. I know I am here with a purpose and until I am thoroughly used up, I will not die. Everything in His time.

This search for purpose is important to me. I have limited time and I feel powerfully the urgency for me to make sure I deliver every drop of my purpose to the world. I did not realise it for the first 35 years of my life—I was sleeping, just like Neo slept in his pod in Matrix. He lived his life feeling out of sorts, not awaken to the fact that his life is not a reality. When eventually he did wake up after taking the red pill, it was drastically different. With my own red pill, I woke up after 35 years and it was indeed very jarring. It was an end to my time asleep and I must move out of my comfort zone. I felt like I was thrown out into the wilderness with very few survival tools.

Finding my place in the world again, resisting the comfortable pull of falling sleeping again, aligning with my purpose and why I was put here at this time with this frame was a long and challenging road. I am not done yet, although the road is becoming more scenic and enjoyable, albeit still a little bumpy. I am clearer about my values and my value. I am still a work in progress and perhaps will be so for the rest of my life, going in and out of transitions.

I am grateful for the rite of passage. The deep inner transformation work allowed me to create my new beginnings and my second mountain as a life coach. Do I want to leave a mark in the world? Yes, I do. My legacy to the world, to my loved ones, is especially important to me. Did I leave this world better because I was here? What are my hopes and dreams for myself? These are questions I am always asking myself.

What I hope for you is that as you go through your own rite of passage and your transitions, through letting go of your endings, moving through your transitions and celebrating your new beginnings, may this book help to give you more clarity, freedom and joy. That you may find your own path, your own dreams and discover the way back to your real self.

May you find the light to the path to really live again!

Acknowledgements

To my family, whose support, love and encouragement, is what helps me get out of my comfort zone again and again.

To my lovely clients and readers, for your trust, openness and daringness to journey with me.

To Sher-li, my dear friend and collaborator, no words can express my gratitude for your continuous support, mentorship and friendship, and your enthusiasm in staying up to read my book in one sitting to write the amazingly inspiring Foreword. Thank you, my friend!

To Lin, Gloria, Toni, Saba, Yi Ning, Suman and Susan, thank you for saying yes to penning the kind and articulate Praises. I am so grateful for your friendship, support and presence in my life!

To my publisher and coach, Kok Hwa and Andrew, your advice is invaluable and your generosity fills me with gratitude.

To the working team behind this book, Zoe my editor, Patricia my cover designer, and Geelyn my designer for the book layout.

To the graduates of So You Want to be an Author workshop (Batch 13), for your support, encouragement and camaraderie as we journey together.

To the Author's Club, for sparking this long-harboured secret wish. You know who you are.

Resources

Books

Bridges, William. *Transitions (40th Anniversay): Making Sense of Life's Changes.* Hachette Books, 2020.

Brooks, David. *The Second Mountain: The Quest for a Moral Life.* Penguin Books Ltd.

Brown, Brené. *The Gifts of Imperfection : Let Go of Who You Think You're Supposed to Be and Embrace Who You Are.* Ebury Publishing, 2020.

Buford, Bob P. *Halftime: Moving from Success to Significance.* Zondervan, 2015.

Chapman, Gary. *The 5 Love Languages: The Secret to Love That Lasts.* Moody Publishers, 2015.

Climo, Liz. *You're Mom: A Little Book for Mothers (And the People Who Love Them).* HarperCollins Publisher, 2020.

Coelho, Paulo. *The Alchemist.* Harper, 2020.

Covey, Stephen R. *The 7 Habits of Highly Effective People: 30th Anniversary Edition.* Simon & Schuster, 2020.

Garcia, Héctor, and, Francesc Miralles, Francesc. *Ikigai: The Japanese Secret to a Long and Happy Life.* Cornerstone, 2018.

Grant, Adam. *Give and Take.* Orion Publishing Co, 2014.

Harley, Willard F. Jr. *His Needs, Her Needs: Building an affair-proof marriage.* Lion Hudson Ltd, 2011.

Ibarra, Herminia. *Act Like a Leader,* Think Like a Leader. Harvard Business School Publishing, 2015.

Kessler, David. *Finding Meaning: The Sixth Stage of Grief.* Ebury Publishing, 2019.

Maxwell, John C. *Leadershift: The 11 Essential Changes Every Leader Must Embrace.* HarperCollins Leadership, 2019.

Murkoff, Heidi. *What to Expect the First Year.* Workman Publishing, 2014.

Pollack, Lindsey. *The Remix: How to Lead and Succeed in the Multigenerational Workplace.* HarperCollins Publishers Inc, 2019.

Singer, Michael A. *The Untethered Soul: The Journey Beyond Yourself.* New Harbinger Publications, 2007.

Watkins, Michael D. *The First 90 Days: Proven Strategies for Getting Up to Speed Faster and Smarter.* Harvard Business Review Press, 2013.

Websites

Dr James Dobson's Family Institute, 2021, www.drjamesdobson.org. Accessed 28 Feb. 2021.

VIA Institute Character Strengths Survey, 2021, www.viacharacter.org. Accessed 28 Feb. 2021.

International Coaching Federation, 2021, coachfederation.org/find-a-coach. Accessed 28 Feb. 2021.

The Gottman Institute, 2021, www.gottman.com. Accessed 28 Feb. 2021.

Articles

Arthur, Dallas. "How to Write Your Birth Story." *The Mindful Mama Collective,* 2018, www.themindfulmamacollective.com/blog/2018/9/11/how-to-write-your-birth-story. Accessed 28 Feb. 2021.

Coughlin, Joseph. "These Are Retirement Numbers All Couples Should Plan On, But Don't." *Forbes,* 2019, www.forbes.com/sites/josephcoughlin/2019/10/29/these-are-retirement-numbers-every-couple-should-plan-on-but-dont/#67e76973186d. Accessed 28 Feb. 2021.

Fleming, Jane. "20 steps to a better LinkedIn profile in 2020." *LinkedIn,* 2020, business.linkedin.com/en-uk/marketing-solutions/blog/posts/content-marketing/2017/17-steps-to-a-better-LinkedIn-profile-in-2017. Accessed 28 Feb. 2021.

Gigante, Shelly. "How to survive retirement with your spouse." *Mass Mutual,* 2020, blog.massmutual.com/post/surviving-retirement-with-your-spouse-. Accessed 28 Feb. 2021.

"5 things to do immediately after being retrenched." *Half The Sky,* 2020, www.halftheskyasia.com/blog/2019/09/5-things-to-do-immediately-after-being-retrenched. Accessed 28 Feb. 2021.

Hall, Nora. "8 Tips to Survive Your Husband's Retirement." *Very Well Mind,* 2020, www.verywellmind.com/survive-your-husbands-retirement-4021742. Accessed 28 Feb. 2021.

Lim-Chong, Sophie. "Choose a Job You love." *Medium,* 2020, medium.com/@sophiebeloved/choose-a-job-your-love-and-you-will-never-have-to-work-a-day-in-your-life-confucius-4825cf7f80e5. Accessed 28 Feb. 2021.

Murphy, Mark. "My Boss And I Have Different Communication Styles, And It's Destroying Our Relationship." *Forbes,* 2016, www.forbes.com/sites/markmurphy/2016/04/24/my-boss-and-i-have-different-communication-styles-and-its-destroying-our-relationship/#4d71c0e38cc0. Accessed 28 Feb. 2021.

Quora. "7 Signs You May Be Ready for a Big Career Change." *Inc.,* 2016, www.inc.com/replacemeplease1456174145.html. Accessed 28 Feb. 2021.

Rampton, John. "Boss Burnout: How to Improve Your Workplace Relationships." *The Economist,* execed.economist.com/blog/career-hacks/boss-burnout-how-improve-your-workplace-relationships. Accessed 28 Feb. 2021.

"Pros and Cons of a Multigenerational Workforce." *Randstad,* 2018, www.randstad.com.sg/workforce-insights/workforce-trends/pros-and-cons-of-a-multigenerational-workforce/. Accessed 28 Feb. 2021.

Yeong, Bryan Christopher. "What To Do When You Are Laid Off Or Fired From Your Job In Singapore." *The Smart Local,* 2020, thesmartlocal.com/read/getting-retrenched-singapore/

Zimmerman, Angelina. "How to Start a Brand-New Chapter at Any Age." *Inc.,* 2016, www.inc.com/angelina-zimmerman/how-to-start-a-brand-new-chapter-at-any-age.html. Accessed 28 Feb. 2021.

Videos

Cohen, Carol Fisherman. "How to get back to work after a career break." *TED,* uploaded by TEDxBeaconStreet, Nov. 2015, www.ted.com/talks/carol_fishman_cohen_how_to_get_back_to_work_after_a_career_break.

Mahajan, Chetan. "Why Getting Laid Off can be a Good Thing." *YouTube,* uploaded by TEDxTalks, 13 Sep. 2018, www.youtube.com/watch?v=MkeaYh4uIE0.

Murray, Brendan. "Retirement: from foreboding to fulfilment." *YouTube,* uploaded by TEDxTalks, 22 Nov. 2017, www.youtube.com/watch?v=CXNQryYDKi0.

“How to know if it’s time to change careers | The Way We Work, a TED series.” *Youtube,* uploaded by TED, 11 Feb. 2020, www.youtube.com/watch?v=_8vLklj_Lsk.

* Listing is correct at the time of publication.

About Lifework

Helmed by Sam, Lifework is a Singapore-based boutique coaching practice focusing exclusively on women with a global outlook. Sam's clients, who are going through life transitions, are often those looking for a better work-life balance, fulfilling relationships, productive careers and financial freedom. They are not afraid of hard work and are go-getters. Through a pragmatic thought-provoking and creative process, Sam adds perspective to and illuminates her clients' blind spots. During the one-to-one sessions, action plans are designed together with the clients to leverage on their full potential. As a coach, Sam uses her experience to partner her clients as a safe-thinking collaborator with compassion, care and energy.

For more info, please visit www.lifeworkglobal.com.

Book Bonus

Do you take good care of yourself? It is often a challenge to regularly do self-care when you have a busy schedule. Yet, self-care is so important to ensure a healthy mind, body and soul.

To help you get started, you can now download the bonus material of 24 Powerful Self-Care Hacks at www.lifeworkglobal.com/self-care.

About the Author

Han Sam, aka Sam, is a life coach who focuses exclusively on coaching women with a global outlook. She specialises in mid-life and career transitions, working with corporate and private individuals in areas of better work-life balance, fulfilling relationships, productive careers, financial freedom, self-awareness, as well as personal and professional development. Her style of coaching is intuitively in the moment, with a creative flair and focus on pragmatic results. Clients love her strong but supportive approach.

Her clients include founders, entrepreneurs, C-suite executives and mid-level managers in MNCs, as well as corporate professionals with backgrounds hailing from healthcare, sustainability management, legal, retail, technology, banking, media, marketing, accountancy, finance and startups. Sam has more than 20 years of experience navigating the corporate world in a NASDAQ-listed company, leading high-performance teams and coaching associates in sales, marketing, operations, as well as support and client management. These are valuable skills she brings to the coaching process. In her last held position, Sam was responsible for market direction and strategies related to the Singapore healthcare market, managing a pipeline worth 140 million dollars.

No stranger to change, her transition from being a pharmacist to working in a multinational healthcare IT company, to starting her own company, reflects her coaching style of exploring the unknown and remaining curious about life.

A graduate from the Coach U Advanced Coaching Program, Sam is Professional Certified Coach accredited by the International Coach Federation. She is also certified as an Extended DISC® profiler. Sam holds a Bachelor's degree in pharmacy from the National University of Singapore and is a Project Management Professional (PMP). Passionate about coaching and getting clients to level up in their lives, Sam was the President of ICF Singapore Chapter (2018-2019) and remains very active in the coaching community.

She lives in Singapore with her husband and four teenage and young adult children, and has her hands full between her personal life and work. The challenges of being a wife, mother, and a full-time worker stretch her balancing skills and mould her decision to live a purposeful life. Sam is an avid reader, gamer, baker, cook, dead lifter and jazz lover.

Calling All Professionals, Business Owners and Entrepreneurs, Speakers and Trainers, Coaches and Consultants, Property Agents and Financial Planners

So You Want To Be An Author

Developing Your Blueprint for Publishing Success

4 REASONS WHY YOU SHOULD BE A PUBLISHED AUTHOR

- Pump up your visibility and increase your presence in the market. With the expanded mindshare you enjoy, you are able to attract more prospects and partners knocking on your door.
- Establish authority in the market without the need to brag. Because book authors are viewed as experts in their field, the trust you gain helps you to convert prospects to better, higher paying clients quickly.
- Build your personal brand and boost your credibility without having to spend thousands of dollars to run expensive advertising or marketing campaigns.
- Spread your ideas to a wider audience even without your physical presence. A book is like a name card on steroids helping you to spread your message and promote you and your business while you are sleeping.

So You Want To Be An Author is a 6-module virtual hands-on authorship masterclass specifically tailored to help game changers like you who aspire to stay at the top of their game by becoming published authors of non-fiction books. In this workshop, you will be guided to develop your own personal blueprint for publishing success using our 6P Framework of Publishing™. This the exactly the same proven framework that over 300 of our authors have followed to take them from just having an idea in their mind to enjoying success today as published authors.

Plan > Pen > Prepare > Produce > Promote > Publicise

LEARNING OUTCOME

- How to identify a niche and develop the contents for a book
- How to nurture your book from idea to market
- What are the critical success factors that can make or break a book
- How to get others to pay for your book before it is even published
- What you must do to market your book to gain maximum exposure
- How to generate free publicity for you, your book and your business

REGISTER TODAY:

https://candidcreation.com/services/authorship-virtual-masterclass/

Kok Hwa's 'So You Want to be an Author' workshop created the spark that gave me the confidence that I was capable of writing and publishing my own book. The structure of the workshop is simple yet very clear and I am referring back to the handouts and my notes regularly. Although I did procrastinate longer than I would have liked, in the end I completed the book and am very happy with the journey and the result."

– Peter Cauwelier, Chief Team Connector, TEAM.AS.ONE
President, World Institute for Action Learning

Workshop facilitators

Phoon Kok Hwa is a Publisher at Candid Creation Publishing, where he has spent the last decade helping hundreds of aspiring authors to get their books written, published, distributed and marketed. Kok Hwa is a literary agent at heart, nurturing and extracting the potential book out of every aspiring author. Apart from his personal beliefs in author expression, he also believes in a pragmatic aspect to publishing a book–personal branding–often stating that nothing produces instant credibility faster than giving away a book as a calling card. Kok Hwa is also a certified as a Professional Action Learning Coach by the World Institute for Action Learning and also a recipient of the International Coaching Excellence Award 2015.

Andrew Chow is a passionate social media and public relations strategist, entrepreneur, speaker and author of *Social Media 247*, *Public Relations 247*, and *Personal Branding 247*. Based in Singapore, his insights into social media strategy, media management and entrepreneurship have made him a choice selection for workshops and public speaking engagements across Asia,through which he educates professionals on how to leverage social channels for business results. Andrew's career has seen him work with an array of clients including AXA Insurance, Abbot Medical Optics, Singtel and Sony Pictures.

ALUMNI HALL OF FAME

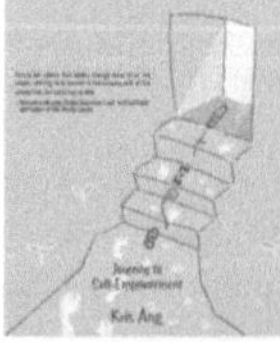

Order your copy today at http://candidcreation.com/bookshop/

www.ingramcontent.com/pod-product-compliance
Ingram Content Group UK Ltd.
Pitfield, Milton Keynes, MK11 3LW, UK
UKHW041955190726
13854UKWH00005B/1987

9 789811 496790